# Pricing Strategy

## Table of Contents

1. An Introduction

2. Goals Of This Section

3. Pricing Strategies

a. Getting Started

b. The Bigger Picture

c. Pricing With Regard To Competition

d. Rule 1: Premium Products Sell At Premium Prices

e. Rule 2: Wowing Through Price Is A Bad Move

f. Don't Be Afraid

g. Time Are Changing

h. Increase Sales by Presenting Choices

i. Rewards For Customers Equals More Cash For You

j. Trials And Lead Generation

k. Banning The Word Cheap

l. Value Added

4. Summary

5. Goals Of This Section

6. Adding Value Explained

a. Cut Off Dates

b. Limited Numbers Done Right

c. Standard Testimonials

d. Testimonials But Better

e. The Ultimate Testimonial

f. The Standard Bonus

g. Bonuses But Smarter

h. Bonuses Done Right

i. A Little Something Extra

7. Summary

# 1. An Introduction

Let me ask you a question. The last time you launched your own product to sell online, or even offline, how did you come to a conclusion about what price you were going to be selling at?

At a guess, I'd probably say you looked at the competition to see what they were charging. While this is a good start, it's far from the whole picture, and you're fumbling in the dark if you looking at competition is the only factor you're taking into account.

Did you know you can double your sales volume by doubling your price? I've done it myself, and I'll show you how.

Did you also know that 99% of the products I see being sold are too cheap. So much so, that they're putting customers off instead of attracting them (which is no doubt what they think they're doing).

Let's dispel some pricing myths and dig right down to the real facts to ensure you get the most cash in your pocket the next time you launch one of your products.

## 2. Goals Of This Section

- To introduce the concepts of fluid pricing strategies, and to show that you have many more avenues to explore than it seems like at first glance.

- To answer some of your questions about how you should price your product for maximum profit taking the number of sales to price ratio's into account.

- To display the effect of pricing too low, where many people price their products without first looking at the all important bigger picture.

- To show you why many people are under pricing their products in a big way, and how you can avoid this pitfall.

- To show you that the price you choose for your product isn't simply about charging less than the competition, in fact by charging more, you can be making even more sales.

- To give you additional pricing options for your main product, and show you how you can significantly increase your profits simply through giving your customers options.

- To demonstrate the correct and most effective way of going about introducing trial periods for your products, and why many get this wrong.

- To show you effective methods of experimenting with your price over time without annoying the people who bought from you previously at a higher price.

## 3. Pricing Strategies

### a. Getting Started

There's some things that I want to talk to you about related to pricing before you head off, create a sales system, put up a website and stuff a price on your product.

The aim of this report is to give some insight into the versatility you have as an online marketer with your own products. The problem is, most people just seem to whack a price on their products with little time spent thinking about it, why they've priced it like that, and what factors are going to contribute to whether it's a successful decision. Sound complicated and a lot of work? Well, let me tell you it's not.

But I think it's really important that I show you just how much freedom to experiment you have with regards to pricing, and what effect getting it wrong can have in a number of ways, so before you put a price on your product and release it to the world, take some time out, have a read, pick up the points and take them into account using them as kind of a checklist.

# b. The Bigger Picture

Now understand, there's a much bigger picture to this than most people realize. A lot of the time prices are put there, just because they can be and possibly fitted loosely around competition and other products and services offering similar things, however, it's not just about planting a number and a dollar sign behind it. All through this process you should be asking yourself lots of why questions. Some of the time, people ask me why the heck I go so in depth into subjects and talk about why they happen. They just want to know how to make a whole load of cash real quick.

Well, I say to them I can tell you how to do stuff, but if the situation changes, and you didn't know why it worked in the first place, then you're going to have to come right back to me again, hand me another five hundred dollars just to find out how to do the same thing in a different way. However, if I tell you how things work, you can take some serious knowledge and know-how away with you, and you have the power to adapt to the fast paced changing world of business online or offline. If you can't adapt, you're dead. Or your business is anyway.

Like I say, there's quite a lot to this, and a lot of things that we're going to talk about, and there's going to be a load of questions that are going to pop into your head. Does competition matter in such a big marketplace with regards to pricing? Should I be cheaper? Should I be more expensive? How do I know when to be which and why? Should I give special offers to particular groups of people? Who? Why? Should I offer different versions of my product at different prices? How do I do that, and how do I know if I'm doing right?

There's a shed load of answers about the above and much more that I'm going to give you in a moment. But all the way through this I want you to keep in mind the flexibility you have as an online marketer with your pricing. Get this right, and it could easily mean double the profits for you. Get it wrong, and it's likely you'll have trouble selling anything at all.

## c. Pricing With Regard To Competition

So with the formalities and generalizations out of the way, lets look at how you should price your products with regard to competition. The reason I want to talk about this first, is simple. When you're looking at pricing, the very first thing you're likely to do is say, hey, so what is everyone else charging for similar products? And you may go from there.

Now there's nothing wrong with doing this at all, but there's more to think about, and a lot more questions to ask than a simple can I beat what this guy is charging for his service?

Your price doesn't have to beat everyone else's out there for you to get sales. This is something that I learned a long time ago, and you may remember me talking about actually increasing my sales by putting the price of the monthly membership up, and offering an option that was actually ten times more money up front, which increased profits even further.

You really need to be aware of what other people are charging for their products, but that doesn't by any means signal that you have to go out there and beat them. Imagine you've just started up an ad tracking and autoresponder script site that's so detailed, and so professional that it smacks the pants off the competition. But see the other sites offering the same service are hanging around at the ten dollar per month mark. Does this mean that you have to go and beat them and have a lower price for anyone to look at you? Nope, not at all. What you have on your hands is a premium product, and you shouldn't be worried to sell it at a premium price.

## d. Rule 1. Premium Products Sell At Premium Prices

So here's rule number one. If you have a great premium product, don't be afraid to bump the price up. You do not by any means have to beat a competitors price to be competitive, in fact, by putting your price up, it's quite possible that you'll outsell your cheaper competition. Why? Simple. Because a higher price screams quality. Don't for one moment believe you have to have the best price to make any sales. That's just not true, you just have to have the best sales system, and of course a premium product if you really ever want anyone to buy from you again.

## e. Rule 2. Wowing Through Price Is A Bad Move

The fact is, if your price is too low, people look at you and wonder why the heck you're charging that tiny amount. If your brand spanking new piece of advanced technology software is really as good as you say it is, why does it only cost ten dollars? So there we have rule number two. Never price yourself so low that you think people will look and think wow that's a quality sounding product, look how little it costs! Because that's not what they're saying at all. They're saying Wow, look at how little that costs. There can't be that much to it, or asking what the catch is.

So in effect, all you're doing here is adding even more value to your product through a higher price. It might be the same product, but I tell you now, it's much more likely to sell more copies at a price that someone might look at and think that it's reasonable, or average than something someone might look at and fall off their chair at how cheap you are.

## f. Don't Be Afraid

Too many people are afraid to take the leap and price their products as they believe they're worth. Too many people look at competition and think they have to cost less otherwise no one is going to buy their stuff, or they'll make less money out of it. This is simply not true. Don't undervalue yourself just for the sake of being cheaper. If you have a better product, you put a higher price tag on it. The experimentation and playing around to find the right combination of offers, deals, follow-up and pricing options can come later.

I could show you so many products that are out there right now, in competition with each other, but one is charging a heck of a lot more than the other. How about this guide as one. Here's us charging you a thousand dollars for the complete set of manuals, but there's plenty of other guides out there that cost ten dollars. Will the quality of both of them be the same? Looking at the price alone, from a customers point of view, I highly doubt it.

## g. Times Are Changing
## Business Needs To Adapt

How about the latest purchase you made for your house, whether it was a whole work surface, a new garage door, a toaster, a dinner table, whatever it was. I bet if you think about it, you'll see that times have changed. A long time ago, even before I was born, people wanted things that worked. They were just ok. But nowadays that's not enough. It's got to be the best, the fastest, the nicest, the easiest to use. There's a real market for premium products emerging. Make sure you don't place yours in the bargain bin if it's meant as premium product, not a bargain basement product.

## h. Increase Sales By

## Presenting Choices

Ok enough of that for now. I want to talk about something else that's rarely done, especially in the world of online marketing and info products, and that's offering different price plans from the word go. Sure people might change their price, put it up and down to experiment, put on offers and so on, but that's not doing much if your original plan isn't well thought out.

Even with the simplest of single sale info products such as this, you're presented with options. The more the better to be honest. Whether you're a high ticket item offering smaller chunks to be paid at extended periods, or a low priced membership site that does the opposite, and offers a lump sum that gives access for three months, six months or even a year.

Remember, the sales process is all about answering the customers questions, and squashing their fears or any problems they may come up with in their minds for not buying your product. It's no good you selling someone on something and then they find out they don't have the payment option they want. Make sure you add multiples of these. It's simple, if there's anyone out there with a website that only offers one payment option, they're losing sales. Don't let this be you.

## i. Rewards For Customers Equal More Cash In Your Pocket

Rule five, and one of the most important. Never ever, no matter what you do ignore the people that have purchased from you before. It's not hard to come up with ways to reward them. Right now, I'm putting together an ID number system for myself that allows previous customers to come along and buy my stuff at a discounted rate.

These people are the most important of all. You've already got them on your lists, they've already bought your stuff, which means they're willing to spend money, and of course they trust you, and they're serious about wanting more information, or the products and services you offer. Remember this, because if you forget you'll go broke. It's as simple as that. You want to keep the customers that are buying from you happy, and you want to stay in touch with them. If you don't go out of your way to please them, you'll have to go out and spend wads more on finding new customers. Look after them, because they'll be with you for a long time to come and will form the base of a successful business from the word go.

## j. Trials & Lead Generation

Rule number six. Avoid free trials unless you're aiming for lead generation. The problem with free trials is that you'll attract all sorts of freebie seekers, and just like I don't want anyone here that doesn't want to make a successful business of themselves, I'm sure you don't want people wasting your time either, taking up valuable resources and just picking something up because it's free.

As I learned with my big experiment site back in the day, it's far better to charge a small amount for a short trial, say one to three dollars for the first week simply to sort those people out that are coming to you just because they can, and those that are coming to you because they're serious.

I've got a great example for you here too. Now a good friend of mine set up a site when we were in our early days on the scene. He had a pretty good product backed up by a multi level affiliate system, or a matrix of sorts. Anyway, he started promoting and all was going well, until word started spreading around some of his affiliates about some guaranteed signups site, that sold signups to anything free, for a fee.

Now unfortunately I'm sure you can see what's coming. Not only did the affiliates go for this one, which wasn't much help to them, because of course most of these untargeted people were just freebie seekers signing up because they were getting something in return from the guaranteed signups sites, and only a tiny percentage were actually going for his hosting package or the pay plan he had in place. What he ended up with was a system clogged full of people that had no idea what they were subscribing to, weren't making him or themselves or the people that referred them any money, and had no interest in doing so. A real resource disaster case that one, because it rendered the pay plan almost useless. Make sure you do this one right and offer a trial for a small fee if your product permits. You could be looking at a similar costly situation otherwise.

## k. Banning The Word Cheap

Rule seven. Never tell anyone your product is cheap for what it is. Yuck. Nothing major to dwell on here really, but never ever describe your products as cheap. Competitively priced yes, the best price for that service yes, cheap, no way. That just devalues your product full stop. More often than not, people don't want cheap. They want quality at a good price, especially in online business.

Rule eight. Don't be afraid to experiment with pricing strategies. I can understand how you might be worried that customers that bought your product costing them four hundred dollars would be annoyed that they receive an e-mail for a special seasonal offer cutting that cost in half, but it seriously doesn't work that way. You're not offending anyone by doing this, and it's the only way you'll come up with new techniques and tactics yourself, through testing.

The fact is real world businesses do this all the time. They have super sales, then they put prices up at Christmas time and particular times of the year when their products are going to be more in demand, discount things daily, add and remove discounts and so on.

It's not a wrong thing to do, it's not unethical, it's business. And if your customers have ever left their houses to go and purchase something from a store, they'll know this too.

So here's the deal. If you need some extra cash, why not offer a limited number of members, a long subscription at a discount of a month or so throughout the year? I have to say this one works real well, and I had a large percentage of my member base from my previous site hand me large up front wads of cash that I could put to good use making more cash. If I'd left them at their twenty dollar per month fee, I might have made an extra few hundred dollars, but at a slower pace.

There's nothing wrong with you adding discounts to the end of five or six day follow-up messages, so on and so forth. Nothing wrong with that at all. In fact, there's nothing wrong with changing your price on your main page without any warning or notice. Don't fall into the trap of worrying what previous customers are going to say, because seriously, this happens in the real world all the time. I know in all my experimental days I've never had someone come to me and shout or complain because I pulled a quarter off the price a day after they bought it. If you have a quality product, that's good enough, not to mention you owe it to yourself to try different methods like in the above examples until you get things dead perfect.

## 1. Value Added

Rule 9. Always add value. We've got a whole section that talks about adding value in a moment, through bonuses, different approaches, promo's, and the like. But for now, remember when coming up with a price for your product, don't let it be the only product. Strange sentence indeed, but look at this way, what kind of things are going to allow you to increase your price and actually persuade people to buy your stuff at the same time?

The quality of your product and sales system are the obvious, but how about bonuses? What about testimonials from known and trusted people in your field? It's not just material things either. What about your reputation and how others see you? So here's a final tidbit of advice for you. If you feel that your product isn't worth the four hundred dollars you're selling it for, then increase it's value through these methods. If you still don't feel it's worth it, then at this point, you know that you're charging too much for it.

Ok, I'll be honest with you. If you want to succeed and get your price just right, without being 'cheap' you have to do a little work. A little research and a little brain work. It's not all straight forward one two three. Understand that it's not about being cheaper than anyone else, it's about pricing your product correctly depending on competition, who you're aiming your product at, it's quality, and your research and tracking results.

By now you should have a clear idea how much you want to charge, and how you're going to go about it. If you have, great. Just remember, the price you put up there on launch day doesn't have to be set in stone by any means. It's there to be tinkered and played with by you until you feel it's correct, and your testing shows you that it's correct. Have a little confidence in your stuff. Next time you create that amazing info product, membership site, or piece of software, try to avoid selling it at rock bottom prices, because I assure you, it's not gaining you sales, it's losing you them.

## 4. Summary

- In this section I'd like to talk to you about pricing strategies, and show you the kind of versatility we have as online marketers with our own products. Many seem to just throw on a price similar to what they think their product is worth, or look at others and try to beat the competition.

- Because our products and the way they're presented is so wide and varied, there's more to pricing your product than meets the eye.

- A lot of people ask me why I go into so much detail when talking about prices amongst other subjects. They say get on with it, I just want to make some cash quickly. Well my answer to this is if It's all well and good if someone tells you how something works, but if the situation changes (which it often does in business, and fast) you need to know the intricacies of why something worked in the first place, allowing you to adapt your methods to the changing situations without having to buy a guide every time new trends appear.

- So how do we decide upon our pricing? Does competition matter and what should I take into consideration when pricing my product? Should I be cheaper? Should I be more expensive? How do I know when to be which and why? Should I give special offers to particular groups of people? Who? Why? Should I offer different versions of my product at different prices? How do I do that, and how do I know if I'm doing right? A shed load of questions and answers we'll be covering in this section.

- So here's my top rules for successful pricing of any product that you create, and the questions that you should be asking yourself as you go through this process, as always from the ground up.

- Rule Number 1. Don't price yourself too low. A low price doesn't mean more profit. When you're looking at pricing, the first thing that would probably jump into your mind if I sent you off right now to price up your products is what is the competition charging? I'm going to charge less.

- Keep in mind from the start, your price doesn't have to match or beat everyone else's, or even come close to doing so for your products to be a success.

- You do indeed need to be aware of what others are charging for similar products, but that doesn't mean you need to beat them.

Why can't your product be the Mercedes or the Aston Martin of your chosen market? It's still a car, but it's the best, a premium product and the price reflects that.

- So rule number one. If you have a great premium product, don't be afraid to bump the price up. By putting your price up and above the competition, you're actually likely to outsell super cheap competition. Why? Simple. Would you expect the same quality from a $10 course as from a $1000 one? So there we have rule number two. Never price yourself so low that you think people will look and think wow that's a quality sounding product, look how little it costs! Because that's not what they're saying at all. They're saying Wow, look at how little that costs. What's the catch?

- In effect all you're doing here is adding even more value to your product through a higher price. It might be the same product, but I'll tell you now, it's much more likely to sell at a price someone will think is reasonable, than something that knocks the reader off their chair at how cheap it is.

- Don't join the crowds who are too afraid to even attempt to bump their prices up. Don't undervalue yourself for the sake of being cheaper. If you have a better product, you go ahead and put a higher price on it. People will soon hear about how you're worth every penny.

- I could show you so many products that are out there right now, in competition with each other, but one is charging a heck of a lot more than the other. How about this guide as one. Here's us charging you a thousand dollars for the full set of manuals, but there's plenty of other guides out there that cost ten dollars. Will the quality of both of them be the same? Looking at the price alone, from a customers point of view, I highly doubt it.

- How about the latest purchase you made for your house, whether it was a whole work surface, a toaster, a dinner table, whatever it was. If you think back, some time ago things were the opposite. People wanted things that were well priced, cheap, and they worked.

They were practical and affordable. Times have changed.

- Nowadays it's got to be the fastest, the best, the most powerful, the nicest, the easiest and least hassle to use. Now is the best time to capitalize on this. Don't put your products in the bargain bin if they're premium products. More on this later.

- Next up, offer choices for your customers. A Pro and a Lite version for example. Not everyone can afford a premium product, and a lite version is just the ticket.

- On top of this, taking the above reason, not everyone can afford premium products, so offer up a choice. Selling premium products is all well and good, but when the price starts to get a little higher, you need to cater to those who can't buy in one go as they may do with less expensive products.

- Next up reward schemes. It's not hard to come up with ways to reward them. Right now, I'm putting together an ID number system for myself that allows previous customers to come along and buy my stuff at a discounted rate.

- These people are the most important of all. You've already got them on your lists, they've already bought your stuff, which means they're willing to spend money, and of course they trust you, and they're serious about wanting more information, or the products and services you offer. Remember this, because if you forget you'll go broke. It's as simple as that. You want to keep the customers that are buying from you happy, and you want to stay in touch with them. If you don't go out of your way to please them, you'll have to go out and spend wads more on getting new customers. Look after them, because they'll be with you for a long time to come and will form the base of a successful business from the word go.

- Rule six. Avoid free trials. Trial periods are often a standard feature for a membership site, but unless you want to waste your time and resources on freebie seekers, set up a limited, less expensive trial for them. A dollar for the first month for example, otherwise you might find yourself wondering why your list of customers aren't buying anything more from you. It's likely because they didn't want to buy in the first place, a waste of your time.

- I've got a great example for you here too. Now a good friend of mine set up a site when we were in our early days on the scene. He had a pretty good product backed up by a multi level affiliate system, or a matrix of sorts. Anyway, he started promoting and all was going well, until word started spreading around some of his affiliates about some guaranteed signups site, that sold signups to anything free, for a fee.

- Now unfortunately I'm sure you can see what's coming. Not only did the affiliates go for this one, which wasn't much help to them, because of course most of these untargeted people were just freebie seekers signing up because they were getting something in return from the guaranteed signups sites, and only a tiny percentage were actually going for his hosting package or the pay plan he had in place. What he ended up with was a system clogged full of people that had no idea what they were subscribing to, weren't making him or themselves or the people that referred them any money, and had no interest in doing so. A real resource disaster that on. Make sure you do this one right and offer a trial for a small fee if your product permits. You could be looking at a similar costly situation otherwise.

- Rule number seven. Never say your product is cheap. It's cost effective, a good deal, but never cheap, which suggests a lack of quality.

- Rule eight. Don't be afraid to experiment with pricing strategies. I can understand how you might be worried that customers that bought your product costing them four hundred dollars would be annoyed that they receive an e-mail for a special seasonal offer cutting that cost in half, but it seriously doesn't work that way. You're not offending anyone by doing this, and it's the only way you'll come up with new techniques and tactics yourself, through testing.

- The fact is real world businesses do this all the time. They have super sales, put prices up at Christmas time and particular times of the year when their products are going to be more in demand, discount things daily, add and remove discounts and so on. It's not a wrong thing to do, it's not unethical, it's business. And if your customers have ever left their houses to go and purchase something from a store, they'll know this.

- So here's the deal. If you need some extra cash, why not offer a limited number of members a long subscription at a discount of a month or so throughout the year? I have to say this one works real well, and I had a large percentage of my member base from my previous site hand me large up front wads of cash that I could put to good use making more cash. If I'd left them at their twenty dollar per month fee, I might have made an extra few hundred dollars, but at a slower pace.

- Rule nine. We've got a whole section that talks about adding value later on, through bonuses, different approaches, promo's, and the like. But for now, remember when coming up with a price for your product, don't let your product be the only product. Strange sentence indeed, but look at this way, what kind of things are going to allow you to increase your price and actually persuade people to buy your stuff?

- The quality of your product and sales system are the obvious, but how about bonuses? What about testimonials from known and trusted people in your field? It's not just material things either. What about your reputation and how other see you? So here's a final tidbit of advice for you. If you feel that your product isn't worth the four hundred dollars you're selling it for, then increase it's value through these methods. If you still don't feel it's worth it, then at this point, you know that you're charging too much for it, and your tracking data will tell you that also.

- Ok, I'll be honest with you. If you want to succeed and get your price just right, without being 'cheap' you have to do a little work. A little research and a little brain work. It's not all straight forward one two three. Understand that it's not about being cheaper than anyone else, it's about pricing your product correctly depending on competition, who you're aiming your product at, it's quality, and your ongoing tracking and testing.

- By now you should have a clear idea how much you want to charge, and how you're going to go about it. If you have, great. Just remember, the price you put up there on launch day doesn't have to be set in stone by any means. It's there to be tinkered and played with by you until you feel it's correct. Have a little confidence in your stuff. Next time you create that amazing info product, membership site, or piece of software, try to avoid selling it at rock bottom prices, because I assure you, it's not gaining you sales, it's losing you them.

# 5. Goals Of This Section

- To introduce concepts of adding value before and after the sale of your product, keeping your customers happy, and putting more money in your pocket.

- To show you how to start looking around you, and to start seeing what other people are doing with their value adding, especially the successful.

- To talk about testimonials and how to take them further to inspire solid confidence in yourself from the customers perspective.

- To look closely at standard bonuses, and to avoid some of the pitfalls of other marketers not in know, who destroy their sales by trying to add value incorrectly.

- To give you three real life examples of real marketers that have tried to add value, but done so incorrectly in one way or another, and to show you how to avoid devastating your sales by doing the same.

- To show that rewarding loyalty goes a long way to increasing sales, and sometimes producing multiple sales from a single product, that means double the profit in your pocket.

- To demonstrate how a simple technique will make sure that your customers remember you and your product for a long time to come, leading to further sales down the line, and nice bulge in your pocket.

## 6. Adding Value Explained

Welcome to the adding value to your products section. You may remember we talked a little about this earlier in the sales letter writing sections, but we didn't quite go into the depth that I would have liked, so I saved it for here instead.

In this section we'll be talking about how to directly influence your sales through the addition of value for your products, ranging from offers, joint venture deals, consultation fees, bonuses and others. You see, it's all about perceived value, and getting the most out of your product. Again, something we talked about in pricing strategies, was getting the price you think your product deserves and persuading people to buy it by stacking on reasons for them to do so, something once mastered will push people over the edge again and again. Pushing them over the edge being hitting the buy button on your site.

Most importantly of all, there's a lot of ways of pulling this off, and they're forever changing, and marketers are coming up with more and more innovative ways to add value to their products. It's worth watching in fact, next time you find yourself reading through a sales letter or some ad copy, look at how they add value to their offer using things that aren't directly related to the product itself. Watching how others do things on their sites is one of the most valuable cost free and pretty much effort free way of doing things you have in your arsenal, but it works extremely well. Keep that in mind all the time, not just throughout this section.

Come back here once you have got your product up and running if you're not working on that right now, because all of these are elements of a sales letter in some way or another, bar two. So lets get started. How about taking it from the top and starting with the most used and widely known and working down to the least widely used, and the new and innovative ideas.

## a. Cut Off Dates

Cut off dates and limited numbers. A great place to start, and really easy to slip into any sales letter for any product. The old cut off dates are probably the most widely used out of all of these methods, and they seem to still be working. All this requires is notification of your low price only being guaranteed until a particular date. These are great words to use, because if you do decide to extend the deadline, you'll find that you can without causing a stir. Way too often recently I've visited sites that say the price will be going up for sure on a particular date, but it never does, and the date magically moves forward each day. Not a good way to be doing business I can assure you. This is catering more to the impulse buyers rather than adding value, but I thought we'd get that in there too anyway, as it's worth a mention for sure.

## b. Limited Numbers Done Right

Next up comes the limited numbers method. Only allowing a limited number of people into the site at a particular time, or only allowing a particular amount of people to buy at a particular price. Again, quite widely used, and both catering to impulse buyers as well as adding value, depending on which method you're using. Now this one I especially like. One of my previous sites has this very system up and running, where I only let a few hundred members in at a time. It's a membership site of course, so reoccurring incomes all around for me, and it makes my members feel a little lucky. Some of them have even told me this themselves, and I've had requests from my list on several occasions asking when a spot will become available because they really wanted to get in.

Now you might say that I'm losing money on such a deal, only letting people in a small number at a time, but it really doesn't happen like that. The reason the limit was set in the first place was so that I'd have time to start working on other projects and could run my other sites on autopilot, so you could say I discovered this one by accident. Don't forget that you can always raise and lower your limits if you do try this, which I highly recommend you do try, even if limiting numbers doesn't suit your situation, limiting numbers on a lower price, very likely will suit every situation, not to mention it always amazes me how far word of mouth travels about this.

## c. Standard Testimonials

Next up comes the hugely widespread and popular standard testimonial. I'm only going to touch on this, because there really isn't a huge amount to say, and I highly doubt anyone out there has never seen one. A standard section of text either throughout your sales letter, down the side of your nav bar, on a separate page or a database of happy customers works without a problem and goes a long way to cementing in your customers minds that your product is good. This is especially true if the person or people writing are well known and respected in your field. Try to get in contact with at least one well known, hand them your product for free, and request a testimonial for it.

## d. Testimonials But Better

That's standard text testimonials over with, so how about looking at the slightly rarer audio testimonials. These cement value in your product even further and increase customer confidence no end. I've personally looked at text testimonials before, and seen some major flaws that gave away to me, and proved without a doubt that they were faked.

This pretty much put a big dent in what I thought of these things early on, and I've even had people come to me and tell me they faked their testimonials in the past. Needless to say I wasn't happy about that. Granted, audio testimonials can be faked too, but it's generally not something that pops into your head when listening compared to reading written ones, hence the big confidence booster and value adding of this method.

If you can get some audio testimonials, whether you ask people to call your answering machine and have them leave messages, or if you're able to record over the net through voice communications, it's well worth it. The extra effort comes in and hits your customers with a massive boost to confidence resulting ultimately in more sales and resources for you and your business. Can't be bad.

# e. The Ultimate Testimonial

Ok, seeing as we've done the audio and text thing with these testimonials, lets go all out, major bells and whistles professionalism with video testimonials. How often do you see streaming video testimonials up on websites? Not very often I'd say. In fact at the time of writing this, I've only seen two in my whole career, and they were great. Real people giving real accounts of using real products that worked. If any type of testimonial is going to add value to your products, it's going to be this one. A simple idea developed into an all singing all dancing, hard hitting method that works.

The next best thing to video testimonials would be inviting these people over to your house to tell you how good the products are. I admit, this is taking things to an extreme, but with all the digital cameras floating around nowadays, and the ability to capture video through the net, and the larger hosting spaces starting to appear through the thought competition, it shouldn't be more than a little time consuming to get a few of these. Well worth it in my opinion. Taking testimonials to the max.

## f. The Standard Bonus

Right, I think we've done about as much as we can with those testimonials, so moving on a little to bonuses. Standard bonuses. Nothing fancy really, all you're doing is offering up some sort of bonus with the purchase of the product, again adding value. Generally these are known as something directly related to your product, or even better, something that will benefit you as well as the customer getting it for free.

How about putting together a small training series that allows the customer to give it away building your reputation, as well as adding value on the initial sale. Or if you're really on a brainy one that day, how about putting something together that will make you money through educating the buyer. For example, giving away an affiliate marketing course to your customers helping them become better affiliates, allowing them to promote your stuff and make you money at he same time.

## g. Bonuses, But Smarter

It's links like this that make up really clever bonuses, where on the surface they might just seem standard to other people that don't understand where you're coming from. Always try to put something together that will benefit you as well as the customer, whether it's increased sales, a re-branded book packed with affiliate links or links to your product they can give away, or an educational tool that will assist your customer, and put money in your pocket at the same time.

In fact, while we're talking about giving away bonuses to enhance your product, I've even seen some really effective products that are just made up of a bunch of bonuses, with no real central product. Of course they have a central theme, and are all related in some way, but this is something to keep in mind for when you've been going a while and having a slow day. As long as all the products compliment each other, and are relevant, they can come together to make a whole new product and income stream for yourself.

## h. Bonuses Done Right

Whilst we're on this subject, please, please take note here, because if I see anyone trying to flog their product, thinking that an e-book entitled ' Doing business today, in the 60's' is going to shift more of their products, I really might have to start wondering about peoples motives. Things like this won't add $500 to your price tag, in fact let me tell you how serious this issue is. If you put a dodgy bonus together, or do this in the wrong way, you can devalue your product so much, that it becomes worthless, and you just won't sell any. Simple as that.

So here's a general rule for you. If you've really thought about it, dug about and tried to find something to add in as a good worthwhile bonus to try and tip customers over the edge and to have more of them buy your product, and you honestly can't find anything that fits the bill, go with nothing or create an original info product yourself. No bonuses are better than one that puts all your customers off. As obvious as that sounds, it seems to be occurring more and more often recently, which is strange, because of the sheer number of people that claim to know what they're talking about that are teaching people what to do with online business nowadays.

Using the example above I want to demonstrate something to you now that also seems to have become a strange epidemic that pretty much makes me and everyone else I know click right off the website and go somewhere else when looking for their products, and that's when people take too much time and put in a little too much effort into adding value to one of their products. Or so they think anyway. Have a look at this one, how many times have you seen this recently?

Example: Get your hard hitting, intensive training course, entitled 'Improve Your Fishing', consisting of two CD's packed with audio and video, showing you all the tricks, tips and tactics in use today by some of the most successful fisherman in the world!. Order now and get this proven course worth over $2500 for a measly $300. In fact, I'm so confident that it's going to help you, I'm going to knock the price down further. You can get all this expertise in one place for an amazing $49.95. Order your copy now!

See where I'm coming from? Don't get me wrong, there's nothing wrong with giving special offers to people who buy there and then catering to impulse buyers, and bargain hunters, or just to show people they're getting a real good deal out of you, but from $2500 down to $49.95? That's going over the top, and unfortunately just makes your product look like a defect.

How would you feel if you walked into a store and saw a top of the range 62" plasma screen knocked down from $12000 to $200? I can tell you, your first reaction would either be 'Yeah right, this a joke', or even more likely 'What's the catch?' or 'What's wrong with it?'.

Remember when we talked earlier about increasing customer confidence in your products, and the whole idea of a sales letter is to squish all these problems and questions people might have with a product, while at the same time creating a want, and sometimes even a need for it. Do you see how adding too much value too soon, or going really over the top can be detrimental?

Where as you see it as giving the customers a bargain, they're seeing it as another question in their minds. Another hurdle that they need to cross, or a question they need to find the answer to before they buy your product. It's everywhere nowadays. Discounts aren't bad on their own, but in this type of circumstance, they are going to kill your sales. Most people don't even know why. If you didn't before, now you do. Don't make the same mistake.

Now one thing I don't want to do is let you think that there is only one bad way to add value (or completely remove value) from your products, because I've seen it done over and over again in different circumstances. I was going to give you three examples here, but lets take the fishing example above as one, and I'm going to give you two more, in totally different situations that will spoil your sales figures. Bear in mind these are real, live examples that are out there right now on the net.

Example one. The 'Only want your bonuses' factor: I land on this pretty blue and white, professionally designed, well built website that immediately makes me smile (Just feels nice when something is presented like this). I proceed to read the sales copy which briefly tells me how I can get money-making tips for free if I sign up to their newsletter. I see links to back issues here too so I'm not really put off by the thoughts of this being another poor excuse to send me ads. Then comes the standard, sign up today and get this freebie. I'm happy, because it looks relevant to what I want to achieve. Now normally at this point I'd just go and sign up, but this person decided to go the extra way to please me.

E-book 1, E-book 2, E-book 3, E-book 4, Software 1, Software 2, Software 3, Software 4,5,6,7 and so on. Now on the surface this might seem like adding value to the point of people not being able to refuse, but honestly, are people signing up to their free newsletter for the freebies or for the content? Again, at first glance getting more subscribers is good right? Well, not really. Not if none of them care about your content and just wanted your collection of fifty thousand e-books. Remember, it's all about quality, not quantity, and this example shows exactly how you can add too much value to a free a product to your detriment in the end. Your quality suffers, so does your pocket, and you've totally wasted your time.

Example two. The 'Not sure what going on' factor: Here's a good one that I see a lot of, and something else that's on the rise too. In fact, to be honest I really think this one is our fault, it's us selling these guides that tell you to sell your bonuses like they're products themselves. This isn't incorrect information, but it can be taken too far.

Again, I'm surfing around the net and land on a site that happens to be a money making op. I'm not opposed to money making opportunities of course, and this one just happens to have a great headline that entices me to read further. The further I get down the sales letter the better it gets, until we hit the bonuses. E-book one, click here to read about this e-book (forwards me to a whole new sales letter), click here to read about this software (takes me to a whole new sales letter) and so on for three or four bonuses. By the time I'm done, I've been taken all over the place, have five windows open, read six sales letters which each try to sell me on to something else, and have trouble finding my way back to your sales letter.

It's important to remember to add value using bonuses in a way which makes your bonuses seem like real products themselves, but never ever lose sight of what you want your website to do.

Don't throw people off in different directions and have them read ten sales letters for different products. It just doesn't work like that. Again while you may think you're adding value, all you're doing is distracting and confusing your visitors. When people say sell your bonuses like a real product, they mean a few hard hitting paragraphs about how this compliments the main product and you're getting a heck of a good deal, or you can't get it anywhere else, or where it's been proven etc. Don't go over the top, or again, you'll be losing customers.

Just these two above examples (three if you include the fishing one) I see every single day, and the worst thing about it is, when people say to me 'Why no sales from my site?' and I tell them that parts of their bonuses sections are destroying their sales letter, I get strange looks and comments. See it's like one of those little annoying mind puzzles, where the solution is so obvious people miss it, and I can tell they don't feel too proud about that, but no worries. Not a problem at all, as long as you learn from it and don't repeat the mistake you'll do fine I tell them.

Now if you've read this far and are ultimately confused or lost as to what the heck you could possibly give as a bonus in addition to your product, or don't have anything to hand, don't worry. It doesn't have to be tangible at all. It doesn't have to be an old e-book (in fact, it'd probably be beneficial if it wasn't an old e-book) it doesn't have to be a piece of software. Open your mind a little and think about other things you could offer to people along with your product. Are you respected in your field of expertise? How about a free one hour, no strings phone or video consultation with your customers purchase, or even a follow-up consultation to see how they've done with the product you've just sold them?

This isn't such a hard thing to implement if you have the knowledge. Personally, I like my free time, and you won't get me talking to you on the phone about your business unless you've just deposited $500 into my account for the hour, and heck, you'd have to know me pretty well and be in my good books to get me down to that price too. Immediately that adds value to this product without me even offering the consultations, because I can tell you now, it took a little longer than three hours to write this guide.

This is something you can do too, and if you really wanted there's nothing wrong with going a step further and actually offering those consultations, maybe 30 minutes or an hour per customer free (depending of course on how many customers you plan to get per week. Be careful not to try to give 100 people a free three hour consultation every week).

You don't have to be in the business of selling guides and info about business to put any of this together. It doesn't matter what you're selling, you can use this method somewhere, whether it's an hour free technical support, or a free 30 minute confidence builder to compliment your main product. It's totally up to you. Be imaginative, and hey, it might even lead to further consultations putting even more cash in your pocket. Again, a freebie helps your customers and you, not just your customers. An important factor indeed, and a question you should be asking yourself when creating any value adding material. How does this help my customers and me?

## i. A Little Something Extra

Before we move on, there's two more ways I'd like to talk to you about adding value to a product. This time though, the bonuses we'll be offering aren't directly related to the product, and aren't necessarily given on the sales letter as most bonuses are. It's always nice to give the customer a little something extra, and this is one way to do that and again, as we talked about before, helping yourself as well as the customer.

The first example I want to talk about is adding an option for discounts related to your other products, either now, or in the future through a ticket system. A good way to do this is allow customers to add additional products to their shopping cart at a discounted price when they check out. Not only does it allow them something extra for a little less, but it allows you to make more sales at the same time, again, benefiting both you and your customer.

If this is the first product you're creating, it doesn't hurt to reward loyalty. How about giving them 10% off the next product they buy from your business? This might not seem like it'll do much on the surface, but when you turn a first time customer into a long term customer that keeps buying from you again and again, this is adding value to your products at it's finest, because it benefits you the most not just today, but far into the future, where your previous customers are picking up two, three, four, and even more of your products within a year.

Lastly, something that's rather underestimated and hardly ever used (at least through the products I've purchased over the years anyway) is again, about rewarding loyalty. If for some reason you don't want to include particular bonuses on the sales letter, why not go for something a little different instead, and hit them with it after they buy the product. Granted, you're losing your additional sales power through presenting this on your sales letter, and instead handing it out after the sale, but let me assure you, if you do this, you will be remembered, and most importantly people will talk about you, and at the same time become long term, loyal customers of yours. Is there anything more valuable?

Above all, if you take nothing else away from this, I want you to remember one thing, and that's that nothing in business is set in stone. No rules that exist now will exist forever, nothing that works now will work forever. The same applies to everything written before you. Experiment, innovate, be different and you will be remembered, make wads of cash and get your name around, and who knows, in six months time you might just be sitting where I am now, typing out a report revealing the newest and most cutting edge marketing methods that you've that you've discovered throughout your journey.

# 7. Summary

- In this section we'll be taking the concept of adding value further, when we look at directly influencing your sales through the addition of value, ranging from specifically crafted offers, JV deals, consultations, bonuses and others to demonstrate perceived value or intangible goods is as good as monetary value with tangible goods.

- There are many ways to add value to your product, and the means and methods are forever changing through new and innovative twists on current techniques. It's worth looking out for these the next time you read a powerful sales letter from a trusted marketer, and asking yourself, how are they adding value to their products? Watching how others do things on their sites is one of the most valuable cost free and pretty much effort free way of research that you have in your arsenal, but it works extremely well. Keep that in mind all the time, not just throughout this section.

- A good place to start here is cut off dates and limited numbers for your sales letters. Probably the most used and widely known aside from testimonials, this one really gets the sales flowing if done correctly.

- All the cut off dates require is notification that a special offer is ending on a particular day, giving the impression that the reader will miss out if they don't buy now. An age old and well used, but effective means of pushing home additional sales.

- If using this method, use the language that shows that your low price and your special offer is only guaranteed until a particular date, this way if you decide to continue to a later date it doesn't cause a stir, and you can avoid using those little java codes that push the date forwards each day relating to the computer clock time at the visitors end.

- Secondly, think about limited numbers. Only allowing a limited number of people into your site a particular point in time. Again, quite widely used, and both catering to impulse buys and adding value. One of my previous sites has this system set up, and still to this day, I have people asking if there's a space open yet, and even offering more money than he standard fee to get in.

- Now you might say that I'm losing money on such a deal, only letting people in a small number at a time, but it really doesn't happen like that. The reason the limit was set in the first place was so that I'd have time to start working on other projects and could run my other sites on autopilot, so you could say I discovered this one by accident. Don't forget that you can always raise and lower your limits if you do try this, which I highly recommend you do try, even if limiting numbers doesn't suit your situation, limiting numbers on a lower price, very likely will suit every situation.

- The next method of adding value is the testimonial. Again, we've talked about this previously, but it deserves a mention. A standard chunk of text either well positioned on your sales letter, or down the side on your nav bar, or even a whole section dedicated to customer comments and testimonials. This does wonders for proof of your products abilities and adding value.

- Taking testimonials to the next step, how about pulling in audio? Simply setting up your answering machine to record, and letting your customers know it's there for them to leave audio testimonials is a great way to add realism and a bit of believability to your customer comments, what's more, they're not exactly easy to fake, so you're inducing even more trust with your readers.

- How about taking things even further with video testimonials. I saw a specific marketer doing this just a few months back, and it made his sales letter really sticky, memorable and powerful. Considering I forget about sales letters just a few hours later unless I learn something, or they're pretty special and unique, this is something I urge you to try if you have the tools to put this together.

- Next up, standard bonuses. Again, lets not dwell on the basics of this because we've already talked about them, but how about taking standard bonus giveaways a little further?

- How about putting together a small training series that allows the customer to give it away building your reputation, as well as adding value on the initial sale. Or if you're really on a brainy one that day, how about putting something together that will make you money through educating the buyer. For example, giving away an affiliate marketing course to your customers helping them become better affiliates, and hopefully promote your stuff and make you money at the same time.

- It's links like this that make up really clever bonuses, where on the surface they might just seem standard to other people that don't understand where you're coming from. Always try to put something together that will benefit you as well as the customer, whether it's increased sales, a re-branded product packed with affiliate links or links to your product they can give away, or an educational tool that will assist your customer, and put money in your pocket at the same time.

- In fact, while we're talking about giving away bonuses to enhance your product, I've even seen some really effective products that are just made up of a bunch of bonuses, with no real central point of focus. Of course they have a central theme, and are all related in some way, but this is something to keep in mind for when you've been going a while and are having a slow day or want to put together a feature packed membership site. As long as all the products compliment each other, and are relevant, they can come together to make a whole new product and income stream for yourself.

- My next point is don't add value to the point of taking it away. Imagine if I tried to give you a bonus with this course and told you it was called 'Business in modern day 60's' and then went head and told you it's worth $500. As an antique maybe, but nothing more.

- If you've really thought about it, dug about and tried to find something to add in as a good worthwhile bonus to try and tip customers over the edge and to have more of them buy your product, and you honestly can't find anything that fits the bill, go with nothing. No bonuses are better than one that puts all your customers off. As obvious as that sounds, it seems to be occurring more and more often recently, which is strange, because of the sheer number of people that claim to know what they're talking about that are teaching people what to do with online business nowadays.

- Next is your price. Have you ever seen those products that tell you that their product is worth five hundred dollars, and then crossed out next to it is a new price with the original crossed out of $250, then that price is crossed out and next to it is a $20 price tag? I think people are smarter than a lot of sales letters give them credit for.

- There's nothing wrong with giving these kinds of signals out to people, but $500 to $20? I don't think so. The reaction is either 'yeah right, this is a joke' or more likely, what the catch? or 'Ok what's wrong with it?' simply devaluing to the point of placing doubt in the customers mind again.

- See how adding too much value too soon, or going really over the top can be detrimental? Where as you see it as giving the customer a bargain, they're seeing it as another question in their minds. Another hurdle that they need to cross, or a question they need to find the answer to before they buy your product. It's everywhere nowadays. Discounts aren't bad on their own, but in this type of circumstance, they are going to kill your sales. Most people don't even know why. If you didn't before, now you do. Don't make the same mistake.

- Here's three real life examples that I've seen of people giving away too much value to their detriment. Number one. I land on this pretty blue and white professionally designed site, which immediately makes me smile. I proceed to read the sales copy, and I'm pleased to report that the free publication sounds mighty enticing. I'm ready to sign up, but before I do, this person decides to go out of their way to entice me.

- E-book bonus 1, 2, 3, 4, 5, 6, 7, 8, 9, 10, in addition to a forty e-book library, software 1, software 2, software 3, software 4, software 5. By the time I got done reading about each one, I'd forgotten what the original product was. On the surface it may seem like adding value, but are people signing up for their free newsletter or the bonuses?

- Giving the earth away is a good method to get numbers, not quality.

- Example two. here's a good one that I see a lot, and something you've probably seen before too. In fact, to be honest I really think this one is our fault, it's us selling these guides that tell you to sell your bonuses like they're products themselves. This isn't incorrect information, but it can be taken too far.

- Again, I'm surfing around the net and land on a site that happens to be a money making op. I'm not opposed to money making opportunities of course, and this one just happens to have a great headline that entices me to read further. The further I get down the sales letter the better it gets, until we hit the bonuses. E-book one, click here to read about this e-book (forwards me to a whole new sales letter), click here to read about this software (takes me to a whole new sales letter) and so on for three or four bonuses. By the time I'm done, I've been taken all over the place, have five windows open and have trouble finding my way back to the original sales letter.

- It's important to remember to add value using bonuses in a way which makes your bonuses seem like real products themselves, but never ever lose sight of what you want your website to do. Don't throw people off in different directions and have them read ten sales letters for different products.

- Two additional ways of adding value. Number one, giving discounts for other products at the checkout. Add this to your cart, and buy them together and save 50%. An excellent and fast way of making double sales in many situations. More cash for you, more value for the customer. Of course not everyone will take up your offer, but the few extra sales sure add up.

- If this is the first product you're creating, it doesn't hurt to reward loyalty. How about giving them 10% off the next product they buy from your business? This might not seem like it'll do much on the surface, but when you turn a first time customer into a long term customer that keeps buying from you again and again, this is adding value to your products at it's finest, because it benefits you the most longer term.

- Lastly, something that's rather underestimated and hardly ever used (at least through the products I've purchased over the years anyway) is again, about rewarding loyalty. If for some reason you don't want to include particular bonuses on the sales letter, why not go for something a little different instead, and hit them with it after they buy the product? Granted, you're losing your additional sales power through presenting this on your sales letter, and instead handing it out after the sale, but let me assure you, if you do this, you will be remembered, and most importantly people will talk about you, and at the same time become long term, loyal customers of yours. Very valuable.

- Above all, if you take nothing else away from this section of the guide, I want you to remember one thing, and that's that nothing in business is set in stone. No rules that exist now will exist forever, nothing that works now will work forever. The same applies to everything written before you. Experiment, innovate, be different and you will be remembered, make wads of cash and get your name around, and who knows, in six months time you might just be sitting where I am now, typing out a report like this revealing the newest marketing methods that you've discovered.

## Pricing Strategy

CPSIA information can be obtained at www.ICGtesting.com
Printed in the USA
LVOW01s1514150514

385952LV00019B/1062/P

9 781497 357884